THE
Gardens IN
GOD'S
STORY

Avows Divine Romance

❧❦❧

MARGARET MONTREUIL

ONEHEART
PUBLICATIONS

Cover by Catherine Reishus McLaughlin

Dedicated to

Wayne Coster Cooper and Jennifer Kaye Masucci.
Thanks for your eagle-eyed proofreading, insightful
feedback, and encouragement.

OTHER BOOKS BY MARGARET MONTREUIL

These books are available through any book store:

Love's Face

✒

God in Sandals: When Jesus Walked Among Us (a novel)

✒

God with Us: A Walk Through the Gospels

✒

His Kingdom Come (a novel)

✒

Writing From The Fire Within:

A Prayer & Writing Workshop

✒

See Page 109 for more information.

Author Website: www.MargaretMontreuil.com

Contact email: mmontreuil@ymail.com

CONTENTS

This life is God's Story.

It behooves us to figure out the reason

we've found ourselves in the middle of it.

From a lovely, loving beginning in Eden,

through the time Jesus lived,

all the way up until now,

God has been dreaming up

something big.

CHAPTER ONE

The Garden of Eden

THE GARDEN OF EDEN

For love, God created the heavens and the earth. There was one place in particular He made that was matchless and quite His favorite. He designed it with an expectant heart. It turned out to be a paradise.

Unlike Heaven, it wasn't elaborate with golden streets smooth as glass, nor were there walls with foundations of precious stones and gates of pearl.

Nor was it majestic. It had no mountains with breathtaking views, no open valleys or rolling hills. It had no massive, commanding ocean nearby, no windswept desert landscape, no powerful waterfall from heights of the earth. Rather, this place had an enclosed, private feeling to it with a distinct purpose in mind.

It was a garden.

God named it Eden, that is, "Delight," and that's exactly what it was for.

The Artist-Creator landscaped it Himself. Green was the dominate color because everything in it was bursting with life. He added an extravagant variety of colorful flowers. Especially nice to hear were the gentle brooks running over rocks, chirping birds, and singing creatures.

He made the garden inviting with comfort in mind: velvety grass, hidden coves under veils of ferns and vines, and gentle breezes carried aromatic scents. You could say it was blissful.

As far as being practical, God created trees and plants that bore delicious, satisfying food. He brought water to the land, carving rivers and streams to nurture every form of life He made. He regulated sunlight for light and warmth, always maintaining the perfect temperature. He thought of misty air to gently water everything. He called forth wind and made sure it stayed pleasant and mild.

God's delight in beauty was expressed everywhere on the face of the earth and in the vast, majestic universe all around it but nowhere was it expressed so lovingly, so expectantly, than in this garden.

The Creator prepared everything, readying the garden just so because the garden was intended for other persons to enjoy with Him even though they did not yet exist.

At last, the big day arrived. The Lord God knelt on the ground and bent over it. Taking dirt in His hands, He formed an image of Himself, breathed life into its nostrils and then called him a man, naming him Adam.

Adam was not like the other creatures God made on earth because Adam was alone, without a mate—indeed, he was made in God's image and God had no mate, that is, no counterpart.

The Lord saw that this was not good for Adam.

God put Adam in a deep sleep and opened his side, removing one of Adam's ribs to form a mate for him. Flesh of Adam's flesh and bone of his bone, God formed a woman to be Adam's counterpart, his equal. She was lovely to the eye and very much like Adam, but opposite in some ways. She was smaller, softer, weaker, more delicate, very sensitive, and extremely lovely. The two of them combined reflected God's image.

Adam emulated God's masculine strength and power, an adventurer, protector, provider; his maleness made him prone to wildness to the point of heroism. Eve demonstrated God's power of attraction, alluring in beauty and goodness, she was sensitive, more the comforter and nurturer than Adam. Both of them were capable of affectionate, passionate love, self-sacrificing as well as receptive. God's affectionate, romantic love found expression between them.

When God designed Eden—it was the perfect setting for love. Besides that, the concept of a counterpart, a "beloved" like Adam and Eve were to each other, held glorious, eternal possibility for God Himself. God wanted loving relationship.

It felt good to the Lord to, in a sense, leave behind

the troubles of warring angels and create what His heart desired.

As far as Lucifer was concerned, the angelic war in Heaven ended by bringing judgment to the fallen angels and defeat hit Lucifer hard. God cast one-third of the angels out of His presence. Lucifer fell like lightning because his place and glory had been so high and brilliant. He eventually earned a new title for himself: "prince of the power of the air."

He roamed about, malcontent, scheming, and proud. Warring against God continued to mean everything to him.

He spied on Adam and Eve from the shadows and saw how God treated them differently than He had the angels.

God gave Adam and Eve one law to keep. It had to do with two specific trees. The Lord told Adam and Eve to eat the fruit freely from the tree of life but He told them not to eat from the other one because, if they did, they would die.

God's only, risky reason for the one commandment: love must be free to be meaningful at all. It cannot be forced or manipulated. The one law and the two trees gave opportunity for Adam and Eve to love God. Every time they walked past the forbidden tree and did not eat its fruit, they expressed their love and faithfulness to God.

Lucifer keenly watched how God had gone to great lengths for them and cared deeply about them. The entire planet was theirs.

Because of the law and the two trees, and God's desire regarding them, Satan saw God's heart as being quite vulnerable.

He plotted to strike hard and do damage where it would hurt God the most. It would be one of Satan's most damaging, strategic moves ever.

When he saw Eve alone one day in the garden, he took the chance to speak with her. Sly in his approach, he sneaked in quietly and appeared friendly and intelligent when he spoke with her. The deceiver implied by his manner that their Maker was holding out on her and her mate, keeping the one tree's fruit from them. "After all, wasn't its fruit that of the *knowledge* of good and evil?" he asked Eve with a laugh, as though she was ignorant of the obvious.

Eve wondered if she and Adam would become more like God, knowing good and evil, if they ate the tree's fruit. Of course, even this question and reasoning meant she doubted God's heart and intentions.

Lucifer told her she would not die if she ate the fruit. Eve didn't know who to believe and gave in to the temptation to find out. Due to Lucifer's ploy, she and Adam both ate the forbidden fruit. Some of what the deceiver said was true. After they both ate it, they knew they were naked.

They'd never been afraid before. Something very bad was happening to them, they feared.

They ran to an area thick with trees when they heard the Lord walking in the garden along a path, in

17

the cool of the evening, as He usually did day after day. What was not usual is that they did not go to Him when they heard His voice calling to them: "Where are you?"

God found them hiding and He closed His eyes, too grieved to see how afraid-to-death they were of Him. He knew what had happened.

Adam answered God while He stood directly in front of his hiding place. "I heard Your voice in the garden," Adam answered, "and I was afraid because I was naked; and I hid myself."

Hearing Adam's frightened voice hurt God worse than his words.

"Who told you that you were naked?" God asked

The Lord reached through ferns and pulled back a flowering shrub until Adam, cowering, stepped out into the open beside Him. Eve came out from her hiding place too. They'd sewn fig leaves together to cover themselves. Their beautiful innocence had completely vanished.

"Adam, have you eaten from the tree of which I told you that you should not eat?"

Adam's tone of voice was accusing, far from a loving response would be: "The woman You gave to be with me, she gave me of the tree, and I ate."

God turned to her. "What is this you have done?"

She, too, wanted the blame to fall elsewhere: "The serpent deceived me, and I ate."

The tree's fruit had opened her eyes to know she had fallen for Lucifer's lies.

God killed an animal in the garden and covered their naked bodies with its hide, the innocent's blood still fresh against their skin. This was repulsive and terribly hard for God to do. He loved the animal he killed to cover their shame.

God's long-range plan to save Adam and Eve and their descendants would prove the best He could ever do for them. However, that grievous day in the Garden of Eden, God embraced the means and cost of their redemption. Animal sacrifice, He knew, could do nothing to remove the power of sin. And yet it would surely pave the way for the Lamb of God who could. God's proving love would change everything forever.

What seemed, at the time, a small choice to Eve and Adam, turned out to be catastrophic from then on. Evil rushed in unfettered into their lives and spread throughout the earth like an unstoppable plague. All of creation felt it. Death invaded Life, and the Hunter found its prey.

No longer were Adam and Eve innocent and free without a care in the world. They, and their children, found pain, suffering, sickness—even murder—the consequence of their deadly choice. They would from then on toil hard just to survive. Weeds sown by their enemy Lucifer would choke life out of their lives and livelihood. God would find creative ways to reach out to help them, but very few of their children would know God intimately in the generations ahead.

With an aching heart, God gave the orders for them to be driven out of the garden. He set an angel with a sword of fire to guard the gate to Eden, which had been their perfect sanctuary. They were not allowed in the beautiful garden nor could they eat from the tree of life anymore because there was no going back once they had eaten the fruit of the knowledge of good and evil.

Even so, God would make things right and bring redemption. But it remained a mystery not to be unveiled fully until after the Son of Man came at the appointed place and time. Blood sacrifices paved the way for God's redeeming incarnation.

When the time was right for the Savior to come, the chosen land of Israel would be crisscrossed by roads, and travel by land and sea would carry the Good News of salvation and God's love with expediency. As far as the Roman occupation, their tortuous method of crucifixion had been foreseen by God all along.

And, like Adam, who was put into a death-sleep while Eve was formed from him so, too, God's beloved would be brought forth after blood and water poured out from His side. Jesus' lifeblood and Spirit would be willingly taken from Him for the sake of His "other." Rather than a rib, the Lord's heart would bear the wound.

God's beloveds would, of necessity, come "from" Him, like Eve had come from Adam. God's spouse, His beloved, would be born of His love and Spirit.

This was God's secret, His future plan, and it comforted Him the day when sin and death came to His beloved Adam and Eve in Eden. God would make good come from it. But it would not be easy. It would cost Him dearly. The tree of life would take the shape of a cross. He would see to it. It would be love at its best, and hate at its worst. But to display love at its best, God decided it would be worth it.

Reflection

In the beginning was God's love because God is love. The Creator has dramatically disclosed His intentions as an unfolding, living story. God's love and pursuit for us have marked the main events in history. This is because God is a relentless lover and is not easily deterred. It is quite obvious once you see it for what it really is. God does not knock once on the door and then leave. Our Creator and Lord is persistent. He takes rejection in stride. He pursues the object of His heart relentlessly. The Most High God made Himself utterly vulnerable for love of us. He did so with Israel for years and years. He does so with each of us.

Ever since Adam and Eve hid themselves in the garden, we do the same. Over and over, in many ways, God calls out, "Where are you?"

Of course He always knows where we are. We cannot get away from His Spirit. God wants us, really wants us, that's what is so hard for us to grasp.

But consider this: there is nothing more delightful than being in love. It's the kind of love that is sweeter than the love between parents and children. It is better than the love between siblings. It is more precious than the love between good friends. It is the best of loves.

Jesus is the King of Kings. Solomon wrote the Song of all songs. There was a Holy of Holies, still is, but it's not in a building of stone in Jerusalem. This spiritual, romantic kind of love is God's Love of loves in the Holy of all that is holy.

God is a passionate lover and has been wooing us since the Garden of Eden. In hindsight, Eden made God's pursuit of love obvious. And, from this side of Jesus of Nazareth's life, we see it much more clearly. The Spirit gives us eyes to see and ears to hear. The Lord is determined and full of zeal with a furious longing in His heart that's willing to do anything for the love of His beloveds. Anything, that is, except use force or manipulation. God woos, entices, persuades, asks, invites, and draws. He gives, reveals, dazzles, loves. He wins us and enjoys doing so. God wants to be wanted.

God's love includes every kind of relational love because each kind of love proceeds from His own heart. He loves as a perfect parent who loves His children. Abba Father. God loves as a brother through Jesus; He's walked in our shoes as one of us. He loves as our closest, most trustworthy friend. And, with the strongest and best of all types of love, God loves as a lover.

Love will always find a way to express itself. We are the object of God's affection. Unequivocally, this is a love story we've found ouselves in the middle of and it is the greatest love story of all.

Prayer

Lord, thank You for the way You have creatively and dramatically revealed Your love and desire for relationship—first in the Garden of Eden, and especially what we learn about You in the Bible. You saw to it that Your love story has been written down. I never want to take Your "love letter" for granted. You have given us everything we need to know and love You, including Yourself—through Jesus and the Holy Spirit. I am alive because You want me. Fan the flames of love in my heart and never let me wander away or outlive my love for You. I cannot wait to experience the final chapter You've been building up to and building up to since the Garden of Eden.

CHAPTER TWO

The Gardener's Seed

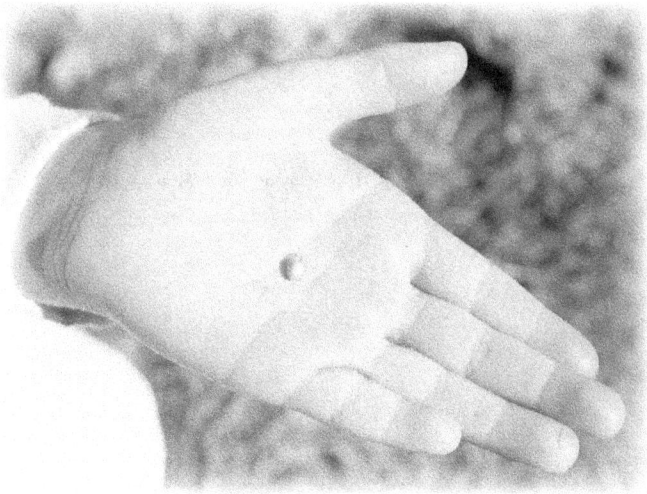

THE GARDENER'S SEED

*A*ngels witnessed the time God created the first seed bound for the earth. Surely, the tiny object was the most mysterious concept the cosmos had ever seen.

Strange, it looked dead in the palm of His hand.

Only a Creator so intelligent and determined to bring life-without-end into being could come up with such a paradoxical plan.

The tiny, humble seed held the power of *life* in it.

The engineering that went into the seed was another thing altogether.

However, God envisioned more than reproduction for this tiny bit of creation. The concept was more powerful than the seed itself. The Creator gave Adam seeds within him to reproduce with Eve. God's greatest joy in all Creation were these two living beings who delighted Him so much. But what happened after Lucifer snaked his way into God's paradise caused an outcry from the heavenly host.

What God had said to the serpent, for the sake of Adam and Eve, became judgment as well as something promising, although mysterious, about a *seed*.

God cursed Lucifer: "Because you have done this, you are cursed more than cattle, and more than every beast of the field; on your belly you shall go, and you shall eat dust all the days of your life. And I will put enmity between you and the woman, and between your seed and her seed; he shall bruise your head, and you shall bruise his heel" Genesis 3:14-15.

The angels reasoned that if God said the seed would be a "he" then of course the seed would be a person, a man. However, God did not explain it to them and so the mystery remained for a very long time.

Evil became like seeds that grew and grew,

covering the earth with sin, hate, and sorrow to the point that God wanted to wipe mankind off of the face of the earth. He made known His disappointment and regret to the angels in Heaven. They wondered how God would keep His promise about the Seed if He destroyed everyone. Perhaps that's the reason it took Him so long to bring judgment.

At last, God found someone worthy to carry the hope of His promise. It was Noah. God saved only Noah and his family's lives from destruction. And Noah's son, Shem, carried the promise forth. God honored Shem eventually through the nation of the Hebrews. God went further and promised Abraham, Isaac, and Jacob that the promised one would come through them.

As time went on, the Hebrew people learned much about being in relationship with the Creator because He called them out from the rest of the world and formed them into a chosen, blessed nation. It wasn't that they were better than anyone else. The Lord's purposes were long-ranged in that their relationship with the Creator was an evolving, living story that had everything to do with Divine love, relationship, and the promised "Seed."

The Hebrews had their ups and downs but it certainly was not because God didn't love them. The children of Israel repeated Adam's and Eve's unfaithfulness quite often.

God never gave up on them.

King David became a person God truly enjoyed. David wasn't perfect, but he pursued God's love. It was a rare thing to be sure. About him, history recorded that David was a man after God's heart. This was what God wanted most. And so the Lord promised David an amazing favor: his seed would produce the eternal king, and He would sit on David's throne forever.

That caught the angels' attention to be sure. And, mystery of all mysteries, the line of David carried the promised Seed up to the time of Mary, a daughter descended from King David. Her husband Joseph, although he did not produce the child, was also from the line of David. This satisfied Jewish law as far as inheritance. Jesus was the Son of David according to law and bloodline.

Heaven rejoiced the day God commissioned Gabriel with a message and a request for the young, virgin woman. Would she be willing to carry and birth the Promised One? The angel elaborated: "You will conceive in your womb and bring forth a Son, and shall call His name Jesus. He will be great, and will be called the Son of the Highest; and the Lord God will give Him the throne of His father David. And He will reign over the house of Jacob forever, and of His kingdom there will be no end" Luke 1:31-33.

This was to fulfill words by one of Israel's great prophets: "For unto us a Child is born, unto us a Son is given; and the government will be upon His shoulder. And His name will be called Wonderful, Counselor, Mighty God, Everlasting Father, Prince of Peace. Of the increase of His government and peace there will be no end. Upon the throne of David and over His kingdom, to order it and establish it with judgment and justice from that time forward, even forever. The zeal of the Lord of hosts will perform this" Isaiah 9:6-7.

Jesus was the promised Seed of Shem, Abraham, Isaac, Jacob, David, and Mary. More important, He was the Seed of God, God's only begotten Son. The virgin, THE woman of Eden's promise, became pregnant by the Holy Spirit.

At one time Adam was like God, now God resembled Adam. What a wonder this was in the angels' eyes. Jesus, the Seed born from a woman, would crush Lucifer's head. They weren't sure how but they knew this much: their sovereign Lord became the Son of Earth and of Heaven.

Jesus lived an ordinary life until His baptism. After that, He showed the wonders of Heaven for three years, turning the world He lived in upside down, preparing the earth for His Seed.

Reflection

In Eden, God's only law for Adam and Eve foreshadowed this one: "Love the Lord your God with all your heart, with all your soul, with all your mind, and with all your strength." God didn't want puppets or to be feared and served out of duty. God wanted loving relationship.

In Eden, God began the bloody sacrifices that people in many cultures have carried on throughout history. Eventually, God formed a people as His own. Called the Hebrews or the Jews, God made sure they kept diligent records of their exact ancestry. He had good reason: His promised "Seed."

God relentlessly pursued relationship with Israel. He gave her sacred festivals, the priesthood, the Law and Prophets, the Temple, the city of Jerusalem—everything God ordained in Judaism became part of God's Love Story. Without the ritual of Passover, Jesus, as the Lamb of God, would mean nothing.

All the sacred feasts, including Passover, existed, and still do, for Messiah Jesus. It was God's plan from the foundations of the world.

The God of Israel wanted to walk among us as one of us like He wanted to do in the Garden of Eden.

One day, every color, race, tribe, and tongue will call Jesus "Lord." He will have His heart's desire and we will have ours.

Prayer

Lord, give us eyes to see and ears to hear. Bring the revelation of Jesus the Messiah, the revelation of the Seed, to the world—that we might be ready for Your return—that the Church will BE a bride, ready to meet You.

CHAPTER THREE

The Garden of Gethsemane

The Garden of Gethsemane, Jerusalem

THE GARDEN OF GETHSEMANE

*O*ur Passover meal finished, I felt strong in spirit—moved by what I had just shared with My disciples. They would carry on in the power from on high. All but one had remained true. My heart ached for Judas but I would not force him to be, or do, what I wanted.

With that exception, Passover was everything I'd meant it to be.

After we finished singing the closing Psalm, I got up from the table and blew out the ritual candles. I peered into the other side of the room, dimly lit, and noticed sleeping-pallets piled against the far wall. Our host had said the guestroom was ours for as long as we needed it. My disciples would sleep here—but not tonight.

I turned to face the tables again. Most of the men were still seated, a few were up and moving about.

"I will not speak with you much longer," I said, raising My voice, "for the prince of this world is coming. He has no hold on Me, but the world must learn that I love the Father and that I do exactly what My Father has commanded Me."

I stepped over to the pegs fixed on the wall near the entrance, retrieved My outer cloak and put it on. "Come, let's go," I said.

Chatter in the room increased and everyone began dressing for outdoors. I stood in place feeling nervousness setting in. This was it. They had no idea what was about to happen. I began to quiet them. "Listen, all of you."

They gave Me their attention. "Before we leave this place, I want to pray and bless you." I raised My mantle over My head to pray. They followed My example. I closed My eyes for a long pause and then looked up to Heaven and began praying aloud:

"Father, the time has come." I looked at My disciples, a varied group of men chosen from ordinary lives. These few would soon be given a life of supernatural adventure.

They had bowed their heads, but several of them stole glances at Me. With My eyes open, I lifted My voice in prayer:

"Glorify Your Son, that Your Son may glorify You. For You granted Him authority over all people that He might give eternal life to all those You have given Him. Now this is eternal life: that they may know You, the only true God, and Jesus the Messiah, whom You have sent. I have brought You glory on the earth by completing the work You gave Me to do. And now, Father, glorify Me in Your presence with the glory I had with You before the world began."

I lifted My palms up and continued: "I have revealed You to those whom You gave Me out of the world. They were Yours; You gave them to Me and they have obeyed Your word. Now they know that

41

everything You have given Me comes from You. For I gave them the words You gave Me and they accepted them. They knew with certainty that I came from You, and they believed that You sent Me."

I paused, drew in a deep breath and exhaled. I bowed My head but not before I saw many of them look up at Me.

"I pray for them. I am not praying for the world, but for those You have given Me, for they are Yours.

"All I have is Yours, and all You have is Mine. And glory has come to Me through them. I will remain in the world no longer, but they are still in the world, and I am coming to You.

"Holy Father, protect them by the power of Your name—the name You gave Me—so that they may be one as We are one.

"While I was with them, I protected them and kept them safe by the name that You gave Me." Looking up again, I placed My hands on the shoulders of Philip and Andrew who stood closest to Me. My voice cracked when I said, "None has been lost, except the one doomed to destruction. And Scripture *will* be fulfilled."

I squeezed My eyes shut. I paused for a few moments. Unwelcome emotions had risen up. When I began again, I made My voice resolute: "I am coming to You now, but I say these things while I am still in the world, so that they may have the full measure of My joy within them. I have given them Your word and the world has hated them, for they are not of the world any more than I am of the world. My prayer is not that You take them out of the world but that You protect them from the evil one. They are not of the world, even as I am not of it. Sanctify them by the truth; Your word is truth. As You sent Me into the world, I have sent them into the world. For them I sanctify Myself, that they too may be truly sanctified.

"My prayer is not for them alone. I pray also for those who will believe in Me through their message, that all of them may be one, Father, just as You are in

Me and I am in You. May they also be in Us so that the world may believe that You have sent Me. I have given them the glory that You gave Me, that they may be one: I in them and You in Me. May they be brought to complete unity to let the world know that You sent Me and have loved them even as You have loved Me.

"Father, I want those You have given Me to be with Me where I am, and to see My glory, the glory You have given Me because You loved Me before the creation of the world.

"Righteous Father, though the world does not know You, I know You, and they know that You have sent Me. I have made You known to them, and will continue to make You known in order that the love You have for Me may be in them and that I Myself may be in them."

Everyone remained still until horses' hooves sounded on a stone pavement close by, awakening us to the present moment. It was right that My final words to them were words of prayer.

I began to tremble a little. "Come, let's go," I said, gesturing toward the door that led outside.

I took the lead down a full story of stone steps from our supper-room. We often took refuge in a garden, which was also an olive grove, just a little beyond the wall's East Gate. That was our destination now.

We used an unlocked gate in the city wall near the estate of Caiaphas and took the footpath along the outside of the wall. Watchmen high in the wall's lookouts, if they saw us, didn't call out because it was Passover and seeing people out and about would not raise alarm on a festival night. Most people were still in the company of their relatives and friends.

As for us, I knew well My men wondered why we must leave the secure, comfortable place, and so late in the evening. I didn't tell them why it was unsafe for us to be found there. Judas would lead the arresting party to the guest room first. I knew that if we were outdoors, they could easily flee. And I knew Judas would look in the garden next.

No matter how much I had warned My disciples about what would happen to Me, they couldn't grasp the gravity of it or the hour. If anything, they were worried about being caught with Me in the city, but that concern had been with them for months. We'd grown accustomed to threats.

I had kept My word to the religious leaders this week. I did not return to the Temple courts. I had said my final words to "Israel" about their blindness and hypocrisy there.

My disciples had come to Me later that day and asked Me about things that would come about in the future. I described key signs and warnings and said many things to them. I knew they had so much to consider and remember, but I'd send them the Holy Spirit to help them.

Tonight, Simon took offense with My prediction that, by early morning, he will have denied knowing Me not once, but three times. He still didn't believe

Me. He lagged behind the others and had said very little since then. I prayed silently for him: "Father, give Simon strength—that his faith will not fail him. Help him overcome the emotional upheaval that will flood his heart with sorrow and regret. When he turns back, I pray he will remember only My love and My faith in him—that above all else. Raise Simon up to become all You want him to be. Yes, Father, for he is My friend, a man chosen, a man I love very much."

As we walked along, silence weighed heavily on us. The moon was full, as was the fullness of time for this Feast, but clouds scudded across overhead and the chilly breeze hurried our pace as much as did our nerves.

The garden grove was just outside the walls of Jerusalem, on the opposite slope of the East Gate which fronted the central part of the Temple. We walked along the path on the outside of the gate and then passed beyond it and downhill to a footbridge.

When we came to the Kidron Brook, it was hard to see the bridge in the darkness. The moonlight was blocked just then by clouds. Still, we needed to cross it. James stumbled into the stream, low now because it hadn't rained for days. The noise of it made Me turn around and I watched Matthew pull him out.

The garden's small gate was covered in flowering vines—beautiful in the daytime. The garden grove gradually rose uphill from here. We were at the base of the Mount of Olives, adjacent to Mount Moriah.

These small mountains in Jerusalem were long ago predestined to be a place of prayer and faith starting with Abraham who was willing to sacrifice his son here. One day, this would become the "New Jerusalem" belonging to the Messiah.

That's why the prophets called Jerusalem married. She belonged to the Lord of Hosts—the God of Israel was both her Maker and her Husband. It is for good reason. My faithful Bride and I will share our love here, a love of Divine origin and eternal purpose which will remain a mystery awaiting the right time. That time was far from Me tonight.

Whenever I came to Jerusalem, it was this olive grove and garden that gave Me uninterrupted solitude and shelter from pressing crowds and relentless scrutiny. I liked to walk and pray along the paths and sit with My back against an olive tree and sometimes I'd sit on a slope higher up and watch people coming and going through the East Gate.

I thought how Eden had much in common with this garden. On warm nights, I brought My men here to sleep in the open air beneath a rustling canopy of tree branches. When cooler, we stayed in the garden's cave, thankful for the natural spring water that bubbled up through a gap in the rock floor.

This visit was unlike any other. Tonight evil lurked in the shadows and the quiet felt eerie as happens before a deadly storm. In My spirit, I sensed angels encamped above Jerusalem—one evil camp and the other holy. Heaven's host would not fight this battle—it was Mine. And about to commence. The garden would not be peaceful and private for long. I needed to pray.

So much depended upon Me at this hour. Every person, every beloved born of mankind, all of them, would be condemned if I refused what I now faced. I considered the torture and shame I would suffer in a matter of hours. It would be inhuman. When Satan influences minds and hearts of people, the horrific atrocities they can do to one another is unspeakable. And they would certainly do their worst to Me.

These thoughts became licking flames of dread inside Me and pressed in on Me until it felt dark and smothering. Judgment had already begun. Even the sky overhead closed up with heavy clouds, hiding the moonlight from Me.

As we neared the cave inside the gated entrance, I said, "Sit here while I go and pray over there."

I asked Simon, John, and James to come apart from the others. Only weeks ago, they had seen Me in brilliant light near the summit of a high mountain in the northern reaches of Galilee. I was glad these three men had heard My Father's voice from Heaven.

It would help them keep faith in Me, for a time such as this.

When the four of us put enough distance from the rest of the men, I leaned on James and Simon for support. I had never done such a thing, I'd never needed to. I began to noticeably shake.

We stopped walking when I bent over, ready to empty My stomach—I stayed this way until the sensation left. I explained how I felt. "My soul is overwhelmed with sorrow . . . " My throat tightened and My voice sounded like someone else's, "to the point of death."

A whirling cold waft of air encircled us. A strangled prayer escaped Me. It was indiscernible to them. We stood together in a circle of bowed heads until I looked up and saw further into the garden.

They glanced furtively at one another and I realized they had no idea how to help Me or what to say. When I saw ahead of us to the right an area more dense with trees, I said, "Stay here and watch with Me." I needed to be alone now but I also wanted them close to Me.

I had to go only a stone's throw away from them to be far enough, where I collapsed in a small clearing with enough space to fall prostrate and cry out.

I knew they could hear Me. I wept, groaned, and prayed without restraint.

I recalled My own words I'd taught: "Unless a grain of wheat falls into the earth and dies, it remains alone; but if it dies, it produces much grain." I took a deep breath and exhaled. This truth identified Me, especially now.

"I am the promised Son, the descendant from the line of David, but I am more than that—I am God's begotten Son. I must die and be planted in the earth.

I waited in the silence, feeling alone, very alone.

The cost was high. What if it did no good? What if I found no faith on the earth in the end? Vivid details of the crucifixion began to fill My mind. How well I knew Isaiah 53 and Psalm 22; these were meant to bear witness of the Messiah's crucifixion after the fact.

I suddenly stood, stretched out My arms, My hands

reaching up to Heaven in the darkness. Nothing. No response. No comfort. Nothing. I buried My face in My hands and groaned. Running both hands through My hair on top of My head, I felt dampness. My scalp and forehead were wet. It was blood. I smelled it on My fingertips, which brought on another wave of nausea.

I must shake off these thoughts. I brought to mind David's Psalm that gave the reason for what I was doing in this garden. It had all begun in Eden's garden.

"Sacrifice and meal offering You have not desired; My ears You have opened. Burnt offering and sin offering You have not required. Then I said, 'Behold, I come. In the scroll of the book it is written of Me. I delight to do Your will, O My God. Your law is within My heart.'

I am praying this prophecy now, Father. This body You have prepared for Me is Yours and I am glad to do Your will."

I meant the words and, yet, I knew My Father and that anything was possible. I spoke out loud: "With You anything is possible. May this cup be taken from Me?"

"Yet not as I will, but as You will." These latter words I spoke softly with My entire heart.

A while later, I prayed the same words. And I prayed them a third time. In the silence that followed, I thought about Abraham, told to sacrifice his beloved son, the son of promise whom he'd waited for for so long, the son whom he adored. I was in close proximity to where the sacrificial ram had been providentially given in his stead, caught in a thicket. Abraham, most relieved, sacrificed the animal instead of his son.

I realized: I am the ram, the sacrifice, caught in the thicket, for no other will be provided. This is My Father's sacrifice, too. I am My Father's "Isaac," God's own Son and the highest sacrifice possible.

An innocent's blood shed to cover sin had started in Eden—the fresh, bloody hide from the first kill. It covered Adam's and Eve's nakedness and guilt. The sacrifice of innocent life for guilty life paved the way to Me, to this very hour.

Because I didn't deserve to die was the reason I must.

An angel appeared beside Me. I knew at once this meant: "No other way." I prayed silently under the angel's watchful gaze. Yes, I nodded and closed My eyes. I accepted what lay before Me.

Alone again, I listened to the sounds around Me. Men snoring. An owl hooting. Trees rustling. I kept straining to hear if anyone was coming. I felt like a trapped animal waiting for My hunter to find Me. Three times I had checked on Simon, James, and John to find them asleep each time. "The spirit is willing, but the flesh is weak," I had said.

The second time I shook them awake, the three of them stared at Me without saying a word. It hurt that they couldn't stay awake knowing My distress was nothing they had ever seen in Me before. When I woke them for the third time I heard noises coming from the garden's gate.

"Are you still sleeping and resting? Enough! The hour has come. Look, the Son of Man is being betrayed into the hands of sinners. Get up! Come on, let's go.

Here comes My betrayer."

I saw Judas. Men and soldiers behind him carried torches and weapons. I looked through the crowd to see the rest of My men coming out from the cave.

With an awkward smile, Judas hesitated and then drew close to Me. He acted like nothing was wrong between us. This was a bitter thing. "Friend," I said, "do what you came for." He embraced Me and kissed Me.

I pulled back. "Judas, are you betraying the Son of Man with a kiss?" A kiss was not meant to wound. My throat tightened and I fought back tears. I searched his eyes for a glimpse of remorse but I saw only pretense.

I moved him to the side to step beyond him and I addressed the mob: "Who is it you seek?"

"Jesus of Nazareth."

"I am He," I answered. They fell to the ground at the sound of My words. I asked them a second time: "Who is it you seek?"

One voice called out: "Jesus of Nazareth!" It

sounded like a battle cry.

"I told you, I am."

The men ventured to their feet and a few of them came forward. A scuffle broke out with swords and shouting. Simon wounded someone. I raised my voice to him: "Put your sword back in its place! No more of this! Shall I not drink the cup the Father has given me?" I knelt down to the injured man who was not a soldier. He was crying out in pain while holding the side of his head. I moved his hand away and cupped Mine over the place where his severed ear had been.

Looking up at Simon, I said, "All who draw the sword will die by the sword. Do you think I cannot call on the Father, and He will at once put at My disposal more than twelve legions of angels? But how then would the Scriptures be fulfilled that say it must happen in this way?"

The man whose ear I restored stared at Me in wonderment while Simon backed away with a stricken expression. I stood and addressed the priests who had accompanied the soldiers: "Am I leading a rebellion that you have come out with swords and clubs to capture Me? Day after day I was with you, teaching in the Temple, and you did not arrest Me. But the Scriptures must be fulfilled."

This caused most of My disciples to run away in different directions. As I watched them go, the soldiers closest to Me seized Me and bound Me with rope.

At that moment, faces and memories played out in My mind. John, his grin the time I called him a "Son of Thunder." Simon, the time he walked on water. Mary, sitting at My feet in rapt attention. My father Joseph, on his death bed. The dear old woman bent over from Satan's cruelty for most of her life, kissing My face while standing erect. My mother beaming at Me at the wedding in Cana. Martha and Mary both clinging to Me, crying with joy, and their brother walking toward us in his graveclothes. I felt love and courage.

I looked up into the night sky. The clouds had parted. Then, under the watchful eyes of Heaven, I was forced to go, pushed and prodded by my captors.

We retraced My earlier steps over the Kidron Brook and back through the small gate near the estate of Caiaphas. They took Me first to the home of Annas who was waiting for Me at this late hour. He and the high priest Caiaphas acted in unison; the charade had begun. My heart was ready.

Reflection

How could a single night mean so much? Mankind sat down at a table with God and, from then on, everything between us became communion. Then Lord Jesus prayed in a garden and agreed to rescue us from sin and death forever. The Passover meal and prayer in Gethsemane were pivotal hours of transcendence. That night in Jerusalem became the center of the Universe, a red pinpoint in the mappings of God's Creation and our history. It defined God's desires and heart. It defined God's history with mankind. It defined the cross. It defined God's mercy and justice. It defined God's love and it defined us.

The traditional meal was more than a religious observance and much, much more than food and wine. From that night on, humanity's relationship with God would never be the same. God closed the book on the Old Covenant and opened the New.

For God, this ultimate Passover celebrated, in reality, the giving of Himself. Afterward, the Lord went out to a garden nearby—but it was no ordinary garden—it was near Mount Moriah where Abraham, in obedience and faith, nearly sacrificed his beloved son, Isaac. It's no coincidence Jesus surrendered Himself in the same area the ram in the thicket had been caught. And nowhere is the humanity of Jesus shown more poignantly than in Gethsemane's garden. It became the soil for the promised "Seed" of Abraham, the "He" who was promised to crush Lucifer's head.

In this garden, the promised Seed died to Himself. Adam and Eve had chosen to disobey God causing death and sin to come upon them and all their children. Jesus chose to obey His Father, choosing His own death to give Life. This act at once finalized God's judgment and brought forgiveness to mankind, redeeming the descendants of Adam and Eve from Sin and Death.

Lord Jesus, the heavenly Bridegroom, walked into the Garden of Gethsemane as the Great I AM, the King of Kings, and the Good Shepherd. He walked out of it as God's Lamb to be sacrificed—for love.

Prayer

Lord, You made Yourself a victim of our sin and hate to become our only hope and savior. Becoming human would have been enough but what You did *as* a human is incomprehensible. What dread You felt in Gethsemane knowing what lay ahead of You. You have won my entire heart. I pray You will find much faith on the earth on the day You return.

An Angel's Comfort

Painting by Carl Bloch

My Sovereign Lord,

from Your Father's side I've come.

And bear no sword or weapon.

On the strength of Your faith,

With the speed of Your love,

In answer to Your prayers, I've come.

Now give all Your love to Your Father above;

No more words, no more tears, only peace.

Yes, lean on me as a Son,

O, Most Beloved One.

The war has begun, Prince of Peace.

The heart of the Almighty did speak,

Through angelic comfort that night:

This is the prayer of surrender, My Son.

Drink from its comfort like wine.

Pass not the dread cup from Your lips,

Drink deeply this choice vintage wine.

Relaxed, folded hands;

bended knees, closed eyes,

Quiet mind with sweet release,

So still while eternity waits.

All silent. All holy.

This moment His glory

Filled me with awe inspired.

With a humbled,

bowed head, in reverence,

He said,

"Not My will, but Yours be done."

CHAPTER FOUR

A Garden in a Cemetery

The Garden Tomb of Jesus Memorial, Jerusalem

A GARDEN IN A CEMETERY

*T*he Romans chose a summit that rose high on a rocky knoll above one of Jerusalem's busiest roads to crucify rebels and criminals, hanging them on display, driving fear into the hearts of passersby.

There was a garden in a cemetery nearby. It surrounded a rich man's unused tomb. The cemetery was close enough that three men could carry Jesus' body down and around the rocky hillside using a footpath that led there.

The men involved in the sorrowful task agreed the entire affair concerning the tomb was due to Providence alone. Joseph of Arimathea owned it. He had bought it for himself because he was getting on in years and wanted to be buried in Jerusalem.

The mount had been a quarry, abandoned about one hundred years before. It served these days as small gardens for vegetables and flowers. It was also a good use of the hillside that tombs be hewn out due to the softer, more forgiving rock.

Joseph's tomb was cut out of an isolated spur of the quarry. The men had to stoop to get through the narrow opening before reaching the inner burial chamber. Here a single burial bench in the form of a shelf had been cut out of the right wall.

Joseph was one of the few Jewish authorities who believed Jesus was the One He claimed to be. He and another leader, a secret follower, along with John, one of Jesus' disciples, carried Jesus' battered, lifeless body to Joseph's tomb. The grief-stricken men wrapped the body lengthwise in a linen burial cloth. This was the one honorable thing they could do. They had little time before running out of daylight and they couldn't perform any work or tasks like this after Shabbat began at sundown. They made it just in time and three women, including Jesus' mother, brought flowers the women picked in the garden. They laid them on the shrouded body. The men didn't realize that what they had done was bury THE precious, holy Seed in the earth.

All of Heaven had witnessed the horror of Jesus' suffering and death. A myriad of angels could have stormed the forces of evil to easily rescue Him. God the Father would not allow it—and so they did nothing but watch and wait.

The angelic witnesses could hardly believe the Most High was in His right mind. In silent horror their eyes beheld their Lord bear shameful, brutal torture.

For that matter, Jesus Himself could have stopped it. He could have blown the entire universe away, could have flown away, could have done anything He wanted to end the atrocity. Instead, the Lord had embraced it with steadfast endurance. This was love that knew no bounds.

The Lord's enemies tormented Him to His

last dying breath. What stamina it took for Him to withstand the hate and to forgive and love in return. This was Jesus' staggering victory.

When Jesus went death's way, His soul and spirit descended to Hades and demanded of Satan: "Let My people go!" Like Moses, He brought them to the "Promised Land," and this happened on the day of Passover.

With excited expectation, two invisible angels joined the soldiers on duty at the garden tomb. Gabriel watched Michael station himself atop the tomb's rolling stone that had been carved out of this quarry. It had been set in place by beasts and much human strength and sweat. It weighed so much it had taken a couple oxen and several workmen to get it positioned in a track for rolling, ready for whomever would be buried within the tomb. The flat rolling stone was designed to cover the mouth of the sepulcher and seal it shut.

The chief priests and the Pharisees had gone to

Pilate because the body had been taken to a burial place.

"Sir," they said, "we remember that while Jesus was alive that deceiver said, 'After three days I will rise again.'" They pressed Pilate to give the order for the tomb to be made secure until after the third day. "Otherwise," they said, "the man's disciples may come and steal the body and tell the people that Jesus has been raised from the dead. This last deception will be worse than the first.'"

Pilate concurred and posted Roman soldiers there to guard the place night and day—until the third day had passed. When the soldiers arrived at the cemetery, they saw that the body of Jesus was inside the tomb and a few mourners were there. They rolled the stone in place as soon as no one was left inside.

Early on the third day, while soldiers and unseen angels kept watch, the ground began to tremble. At once, Michael appeared in brilliance to the soldiers and rolled the stone away and then sat down on it again.

The guards were so afraid of him they began shaking and fell prostrate until they gained enough wits and courage to run away.

Michael and Gabriel anticipated Jesus to rise at the crack of dawn and they were right. This was the dawn of a new day, and the trembling ground soon began to quake. It was then they saw brilliant light shine out from the cavity of the sepulcher. When the ground stopped shaking, their Sovereign Lord stepped out, took a deep breath, and rewarded them with a smile. The angels worshiped Him with ecstatic joy. Jesus was radiant, dressed in white attire, and His face beamed— their Lord in His glory was back!

Mary Magdalene's main concern on her way to the garden tomb was how she would get beyond the rolling stone. When she arrived, she was relieved to see the rolling stone positioned to the side of the sepulchre's opening. She would be able to go in to Jesus. She knew soldiers had been stationed outside the tomb but she saw no one. She didn't know Jesus was the only man left there.

The soldiers had run off and two angels were inside the sepulcher, ready with messages for anyone who came in. Other women had just been there and Michael and Gabriel had sent them off with the glorious news that Jesus had risen.

Now it was Mary's turn. However, Jesus wanted to surprise her Himself, so the angels did not appear to her at first.

Jesus watched Mary stoop down and peer into the tomb. There was just enough light for her to see the body was not there. She dropped the fragrant spices she'd brought on the ground and took her skirt in both hands and hurried away.

Jesus knew she ran as fast as she could to the guest room where the Eleven were gathered. It was remarkable, considering the distance, how soon she returned with Simon and John in tow.

With love and delight, Jesus watched them enter the tomb and reappear outside of it with bewildered expressions. Simon bore grief and apprehension— he still felt ashamed for denying his Lord. John had become like a small child, excited and filled with wonder. The two of them hurried back to the others in Jerusalem.

Mary stayed. She could not bring herself to leave. Jesus marveled at this, soaking up the entire scene and determined not to let her cry too much longer.

He watched with love as she sat down and leaned against the stone that had been rolled away. She continued to cry. Tears alone expressed her sorrow for a little while. He knew all of her thoughts.

Mary remembered looking up at Jesus from the foot of the cross. She had gazed with horror and despair at His feet and hands, spikes holding Him to the wood. Then she recalled His hands gesturing while teaching, patting her on the head, squeezing her hand to show her His thanks for something she'd done . . . His kind, life-giving, beautiful hands.

Overcome by her thoughts, she jumped to her feet. She must see His hands one last time. Even lifeless, she wanted to touch them again, even if she could only touch the burial cloth that covered them. How could she live without Him? How could she bear to never hear His voice again? He was the only man who had ever known her, ever made her feel acceptable and truly cared for. She stepped to the sepulcher's opening and stooped to peer into its cavity once more. She went further in when she saw movement.

She saw two men, dressed in white, who had not been there before. One of them asked her, "Woman, why are you crying?"

"They have taken my Lord away," she said, "and I don't know where they have put Him."

Jesus stepped up to the mouth of the tomb but He did not stoop down.

"Woman, why are you crying?" Jesus asked. "Who

is it you are looking for?"

She glanced back and saw Him from the shoulders down. She assumed He was the gardener. Also, she was preoccupied with angels, although she didn't know they were angels.

"Sir," she said, to the man just outside the cave's entrance, "if you have carried Him away, tell me where you have put Him, and I will get Him."

Jesus saw her love for Him caused her to lose all logic. How could this frail woman carry a man's body? Her desperate love for Him endeared Him so much He couldn't keep His secret a moment longer.

"Mary." Somehow His entire heart full of love for her sounded in her name.

She turned all the way around and moved out from the opening of the sepulcher and ended up standing face to face with Him. She blurted, "Rabboni!" and wrapped her arms around Him and held Him fast.

He laughed a soft laugh. He realized she would

not let go on her own. "You mustn't cling to Me," He said.

She pulled away and He looked into her eyes. "I haven't yet returned to the Father," He said.

She stepped further back, nodding and smiling. Now tears of joy, not sorrow, streamed down her face.

"Go instead to my brothers and tell them, I am returning to My Father and your Father, to My God and your God."

She covered her mouth with both hands like a young girl would stifle an outburst of delight. She was so thrilled to see Him.

Smiling, He gestured for her to go while nodding in encouragement. As Jesus watched her go, a thought occurred to Him: this garden was as delightful as Eden had ever been—even more so—and this was just the beginning.

Reflection

The Lord's powerful display of glory came after succumbing to everything hell could do to Him. Satan "bruised His heel." As for the curse on mankind—Jesus became the perfect atonement, redeeming believers from all sin and death. This turned everything on Satan's head and crushed him. Out of Death came Life. This was no ordinary "seed" and only God could have done such a thing.

Besides, a garden is meant for the living, not the dead. How beautiful the garden when, at last, God had His heart's desire.

Prayer

I am in awe of You, Lord, but to think You acted so human in the garden, savoring the moment of Your greatest surprise. It shows what You hold in Your heart for a single soul. Even today, Your beloveds wish to put themselves in Mary's sandals. You first revealed

Your glorious self to the one longing for You. We want to experience that kind of love with You, too. Precious Jesus, You are more wonderful than words can express. A soul who seeks You for You alone is a soul longing to hear You whisper their own name in their ear. There is no greater thing in life than that.

God's Son, the Promised Seed

God breathed life into the first man.
He created Eve from Adam's rib.
But what was the meaning of the Seed
God promised He would send?

Jesus was the Seed of God.
All the angels knew.
But what in the world, they wondered,
Did their Sovereign plan to do?

Once Jesus told His men,
That a seed must surely die,
And then be planted in the earth,
To yield an abundance of like kind.

Thorns and Kisses

God's broken heart spoke words in Eden
to curse the ground.
Thorns would come and pierce our lives
and His own.
We'd toil in the sun and die,
God's face forbidden.
Till Jesus, King of Heaven,
came down, beneath the scorching sun,
our sins at last forgiven.

To think we crowned Him king
with cursing thorns,
God's face and brow the ground.
O, piercing thorns, your victim has Himself
redeemed us back to Eden,
to live forever
in the garden of Heaven.

Till then, we kiss His face and brow,
in the garden of our love.

CHAPTER FIVE

A Spiritual Garden of Delight

A SPIRITUAL GARDEN OF DELIGHT

*C*ome, cling to Jesus in this new, living way. We are invited to once again eat from the tree of life. No longer is an angel posted outside its gate to keep us out. God invites us to partake of eternal life, to enjoy knowing Him in spiritual reality and in Truth. This is the *Love of all loves* with the *King of all kings* in the *Holy of all that is holy*.

The following Scriptures and poems are provided as a means to meet the Divine Bridegroom in a spiritual garden—this is a "Garden of Delight."

As the Psalmist penned words regarding the Messiah, let us take up his song: "Lift up your gates (your hearts) ye everlasting doors, and let the Lord of glory come in!"

This inner sanctuary, as the Song of Songs so aptly describes, is for Jesus and His beloved. Jesus sings the words to the one He passionately loves:

"I have come to My garden, My sister,

My spouse;

I have gathered My myrrh with My spice;

I have eaten My honeycomb with My honey;

I have drunk My wine with My milk.

Eat, O friends!

Drink, yes, drink deeply, O beloved ones!"

Song of Solomon 5:1, NKJV

We have entered into a love affair with our Lord. It is God who receives the fruit of a believer's life and love. Here the Father, Jesus, and the Holy Spirit enjoy the delightful good in this garden, a garden which has matured in their beloved one.

"A garden enclosed is My sister, My spouse,

A spring shut up, a fountain sealed.

Your plants are an orchard of pomegranates

With pleasant fruits,

Fragrant henna with spikenard,

Spikenard and saffron, calamus and cinnamon,

With all trees of frankincense,

Myrrh and aloes,

With all the chief spices—a fountain of
gardens,

A well of living waters,

And streams flowing from Lebanon."

Song of Solomon 4:12-15, NKJV

It is here the Lord of Glory comes and drinks of the wine of joy and tastes its sweetness like honey. He picks and eats the fruit of their love. Here within this one is living water flowing from His Spirit. The Lord's beloved one has become a well of living waters, flowing with movement, never stagnant. It is so wonderful to think that we can affect God's heart and bring Him joy. The bride says:

> "My Beloved has gone to His garden,
>
> To the beds of spices,
>
> To feed His flock in the gardens,
>
> And to gather lilies.
>
> I am my Beloved's and my Beloved is mine.
>
> He feeds His flock among the lilies."
>
> *Song of Solomon 6:2-3, NKJV*

We share the company of the Bridegroom while He abides in our Garden of Delight. It is an inner experience. The ultimate Divine love relationship in this garden is for God and His bride/spouse alone.

"The voice of my Beloved!

Behold, He comes, leaping upon mountains,

Skipping upon the hills,

My Beloved is like a gazelle or a young stag.

Behold, He stands behind our wall;

He is looking through the windows,

Gazing through the lattice.

My Beloved spoke, and said to me:

'Rise up, My love, My fair one,

And come away.'"

Song of Solomon 2:8-10, NKJV

"Behold, you *are* fair, My love!

Behold, you *are* fair!

You *have* dove's eyes behind your veil."

Song of Solomon 4:1a, NKJV

You and I, individually, are this fair, loved one. Why does our Lord see His beloved one as lovely? It is because of the cross. This may have happened in the past, but it is in the constant present. We are being saved every day by Jesus' sacrificial, atoning death on the cross.

This act of the Lord was love in its highest form. Our sins hammered nails into Jesus' hands and feet as surely as did His executioners. We can't blame the Jewish authorities or the Romans. Our sins brought Jesus to the cross. God made a way to save each one of us. The men responsible for judging Him and killing Him were no different than any of us. Like them, we have hurt God many times. We've misjudged our Lord's heart towards us in areas we hardly realize.

His heart was pierced through to prove death. And the water and blood that poured out from His side made it possible for Him to have a counterpart. We can be His "beloved" forever.

And now God says that only the righteousness of His Son remains in "her." He sees the believer's faith and devotion. All along God wanted a beloved one, someone to share His Life with Him as His "Other."

His suffering and death brought "her" to love Him.

And now the Lord wants His loved one to come with Him. He draws one's soul to come after Him—to come away with Him.

"My beloved spoke, and said to me:

'Rise up, My love, My fair one,

And come away.

For lo, the winter is past,

The rain is over and gone.

The flowers appear on the earth;

The time of singing has come,

And the voice of the turtledove

Is heard in our land.'"

Song of Solomon 2:10-12, NKJV

What does it mean that the voice of the turtledove has been heard in our land? Spring is a time of new beginnings and love blooms after a long wait.

God says to His beloved, "You have dove's eyes."

Doves mate for life, staying with one, or none. Doves have singular vision which means they have "eyes for only one thing at a time." The Lord's beloved has spiritual eyes for Him.

"Blessed are the pure in heart for they will see God." To have singular vision for God is to have a pure heart. The reward of purity of heart is life within the Holy of Holies, intimacy beyond the veil.

It is union with Jesus. "He brought me into His chambers," the Song of Songs proclaims. This is how God designed us to be.

The Lover calls His beloved a dove throughout the Song. God is calling His mate into intimacy.

Have you ever watched a pair of doves together? They stay close to each other, they coo and call to each other. They cuddle.

Of course, for us to "cuddle" with God means we have to first "cling" to Him. He wants to be in a love relationship with us. This is that unique love—God's desire for us. It certainly is a mystery but one we can experience. Just as Adam *knew* Eve, God made a way for His heart and love to be expressed.

Faith is nothing if not a love affair with God. Grace is the only way it can begin. God draws us first. Desire is our way of responding. It is what brings us close. God spoke through a prophet: "Seek Me with all of your heart and you will find Me" Jeremiah 29:11. God enjoys the pursuit—it's the way of love.

God's Spirit will lead us to the cleft in the rock, which is in a very steep place. It is not found on a path well traveled.

When the bride first begins to love God for who He is and not only for what He can do, a new vibrant flame of passion ignites between them. Like Moses, we want more than anything to see God's face, to see God's glory. God wants this, too. This is Divine romance.

Reflection

God invites us to know Him as the lover of our soul. God's Story on earth is the unfolding of the Lord's great pursuit for a counterpart.

It's easier to think this means a "corporate" counterpart. It's that and more. God wants intimacy with His own beloved, a heartfelt "being in love" relationship that can only be shared one-on-one.

Dare to believe. As redeemed believers, we are betrothed to the Lord, our heavenly Bridegroom prophets have revealed throughout the ages in Scripture. God longs for the marriage's consummation. This spiritual union involves one's inner person: our heart, mind, and soul. God is Spirit and spiritual just as God is Love and loving. The Creator of the Universe wants to be as intimate with us as does a lover and his beloved on the night of their wedding. This also means the glorified Lord Jesus wants to be in union with us as though married, sharing our lives and assets as one.

We must consider the lengths the Lord has gone to to relinquish everything to win us, to convince us, to enjoy us. We are the reason God made Himself vulnerable, not only to rejection and a gruesome death, but to love. God is willing to be rejected by everyone born. He waits for love to awaken in us. Sometimes it never does. True vulnerability and openness for both parties is crucial in a love relationship. It's hard to grasp that it is God who wants this. A "passionate lover" describes God best.

Religion is a word we use to describe that part of our lives partitioned off for our faith. Jesus hates religion. What God wants is to own us and be owned by us. He's too much a lover to want anything less.

"Many will say to Me on that day, 'Lord, Lord, did we not prophesy in Your name, and in Your name drive out demons and perform many miracles?' Then I will tell them plainly, 'I never knew you. Away from Me, you evildoers!'" (Matthew 7:22-23.)

"The Spirit and the bride say, 'Come!' And let him who hears say, 'Come!' And let him who thirsts come."

Oh, to love the way God loves. If we open the garden gate in our heart, the Lord of glory will come in.

Prayer

Lord, You are everything *Good* I have ever wanted. You are wonderful beyond any words I can say. I want to delight You and *know* You as You know me. Lord Jesus, all of Creation longs for Your return to the earth. Thank you for Your love and all You've done for me.

O My dove, in the clefts of the rock,

In the secret *places* of the cliff,

Let Me see your face,

Let Me hear your voice;

For your voice is sweet,

And your face is lovely."

Song of Solomon 2:14, NKJV

A Song of the Bridegroom & the Bride

Bridegroom:

Come within, I bid you, come
Inside this secret chamber deep
In the place of your own heart
Is where we two should meet

Remove the veil
There's no more need
And let Me see your face
In this secret, holy place

Bride:

My Lord, I dare not
For I have sinned
Ashamed and full of need I am
Your cross has just begun its work
Not yet complete in me

Bridegroom:

We have made for you

Garments, rich

A wedding gown, white

Trimmed with gold

We adorn you with silver chains

Rubies and precious jewels

All these we've given you

My lovely bride, to wear

Bride:

Beautiful Lord, I am not worthy

But Your eyes with kindness shine

And all the dark and lonely aches

Depart as love imparts

Your glory in my heart

Your costly blood-grown wine

Rich and vibrant to my taste

It goes down smooth and lifts

My soul now deeply blessed

I soar higher than before

I'm filled with love and life

Across the timeless fathoms

His Majesty has reached

And bent so low to kiss

The one He loves

And spent Himself to make us one

In bliss, You fill my soul

Your kiss is so much more

Than can be told

And sweet Your breath, so near

Life's deepest joy to know

EPILOGUE

Heaven's Garden of Eden

HEAVEN'S GARDEN OF EDEN

Our Creator made angels long before He made people, so God's larger story began before we became part of it. The Garden of Eden on Earth was *our* beginning but not *the* beginning of God's epic drama.

Eden is mentioned in the Scriptures as being a sacred garden in Heaven where Lucifer came in and went out before his betrayal and fall.

"And there was war in Heaven" Revelation 12:7 indicates the magnitude of Lucifer's wrongdoing.

God's Lamentation for Lucifer

"You *were* the seal of perfection,

Full of wisdom and perfect in beauty.

You were in Eden, the garden of God;

Every precious stone was your covering:

The sardius, topaz, and diamond,

Beryl, onyx, and jasper,

Sapphire, turquoise, and emerald with gold.

The workmanship of your timbrels and pipes

Was prepared for you on the day you were created.

"You were the anointed cherub who covers;

I established you;

You were on the holy mountain of God;

You walked back and forth in the midst of fiery stones.

You were perfect in your ways from the day you were

created,

Till iniquity was found in you."

Ezekiel 28:12-15, NKJV

After the war in Heaven, could it be that God decided to create beings who would love as He loved? Afterall, romantic, espousal love originated in God's heart.

God set out on a magnificent quest knowing from the outset it would mean sacrifice, risk, vulnerability, rejection, loss, and pain. He saw ahead to His reward and decided it would be worth it.

That is the sum of it: we were worth it to Him.

Now we know, God will do anything to woo us, to create love in us. What Jesus did on the cross for us showed us the extent of His love. He came not just to die for our sins but to prove the extent of His love.

Ultimately, God wants His beloveds of Earth to join Him in the the Garden of Eden in Heaven.

He determined to create a loving mate for Himself, one to reign with Him side by side. Chosen. Adorned. Wanted. Enjoyed. God wants to be *wanted* by the ones He wants. He WON us to Himself. We are His reward and joy. And He is ours.

105

God once loved and adorned Lucifer. We can't begin to imagine what the angel gave up when he turned against God in his pride. He fell from the glory of God and Heaven like a falling star. Lucifer will never again see Heaven's Eden. Nor will he walk among the fiery stones.

We are God's beloveds. Once we arrive in the Garden of Eden in Heaven, we will know nothing but glorious, adoring love. We will dance among the fiery stones and call God's holy mount in Heaven our home. God will adorn us with gemstones and anoint us for who we truly are.

Nothing will ever again come between *God and His Beloveds* and yearning and sorrow will be no more.

ABOUT THE AUTHOR

Margaret Montreuil is an artist who paints portraits of Jesus with words and sees God's larger love story as a Divine epic we are part of.

An insatiable desire to know God drew Margaret to meditate for many years on the humanity of Jesus in the Gospels. She embraced our Jewish roots of Christian faith because they define Jesus, us, and where we're going. Far from being a religious personality, her portrayal of Jesus is relevant, an unstoppable force of unleashed love, the Messiah fulfilling destiny. Margaret knows that happy reading is to dive headlong into a transcendent experience — and she cannot think of a better ocean than the love of God as portrayed by Jesus.

Margaret teaches others about prayer and

facilitates spiritual retreats. The mother of five adult children and a grandmother of five grandchildren, Margaret lives in Charlotte, North Carolina.

Feel free to connect with Margaret through her website at: www.margaretmontreuil.com. Be sure to subscribe there to receive email notifications for her inspirational blogs and news of upcoming projects.

Available to order in any book store.

Love's Face is an inspirational book about Jesus as the Lover of the soul.

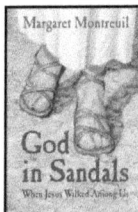

God in Sandals: When Jesus Walked Among Us is a biblically-based novel on the life of Jesus. Available in dramatic audio, e-book, and print formats.

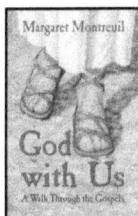

God with Us: A Walk through the Gospels is a companion to *God in Sandals* as well as a stand-alone inspirational book on the life of Jesus that follows a harmony of the Gospels.

His Kingdom Come is a biblically-based novel that continues the story where *God in Sandals* leaves off. The timeframe is the first several years in Jerusalem at the birth of the Church.

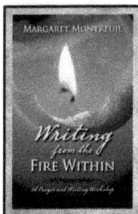

Writing from the Fire Within: A Prayer & Writing Workshop is for Christians to experience listening prayer, reflection, journaling, and writing to inspire.

www.ingramcontent.com/pod-product-compliance
Lightning Source LLC
Chambersburg PA
CBHW071639050426
42443CB00026B/736